T0363818

Build a Smokehouse

CONTENTS

Introduction

Some of the most mouth-watering, epicurean delights in gourmet stores are smoked hams, breasts of turkey, pheasants, eels, salmon, whitefish, and trout. These delicacies are also very, very expensive, and most of us buy them in miniscule amounts for special occasions. But if you have your own smokehouse, you can enjoy these luxuries and dozens of superbly flavored foods from smoked homemade sausages, venison, beef, and lamb, to wild game birds, clams, oysters, shrimp, squid, and freshwater fish. If you fish or hunt or farm livestock, your costs will be a fraction of what you might pay at the delicatessen counter. But there are other sound reasons for building a smokehouse and smoking your own products.

- If you raise your own poultry, porkers, or bullpout, curing and smoking is yet another way to preserve the meat, far more delicious than freezing or canning it.
- People with smokehouses tend to raise stock themselves, especially for smoking, giving them great independence and self-sufficiency. Range-fed chickens or turkeys hatched in the spring, then killed in late autumn, cured, and smoked at home, are a very inexpensive form of protein.
- A smokehouse can be a community resource that draws rural neighbors together and motivates more people to raise their own meat animals. If you build a smokehouse, share it with others. You can barter the use of your smokehouse for smoker hardwood or a share of the finished meat.
- Much fish and game, hard-won from river and field, go to waste because they are poorly prepared or unappealing to our overcivilized palates. Smoking mellows and enriches the flavor as well as preserves the meat. Once you have learned the techniques of smoking, you can rig up a simple smokehouse on a fishing or hunting trip and preserve your catch in the field.

In recent years dozens of commercial smokers have appeared on the market, most of them expensive, hard to clean, and none of them more efficient than a homemade smoker. You can make a simple smoke box or barrel that works very well, or you can build a strong, tight smokehouse that will endure for decades. In southern hog-raising country, smokehouses a century old are still doing service.

What Is Smoking?

Smoking is an ancient food preservation technique that probably goes back to the first delighted efforts of human beings to cook meat and fish over fire. Smoking lowers the moisture content of food and seals the exterior with a hard, golden-brown film; the complex chemical reactions between the smoke, the meat protein, and the internal moisture inhibit the growth of undesirable microorganisms. The temperature of the heated air that accompanies the smoke, the construction and venting of the smoker, the length of time the meat is exposed to the heat and smoke, as well as the slightly different flavors given off by various woods, all contribute to the unique tastes, textures, and keeping qualities of each smoked food product. Although early adventures with smoking your own foods can give highly variable results, eventually you learn how long, what wood, and what temperatures with what foods suit your palate best.

Early people discovered that brining or curing meat in a salt solution before smoking it removed more moisture from the protein tissue and greatly enhanced both the preservative characteristics and the flavor of the meat. Over the centuries, three basic ways of curing and/or smoking meats, fish, and poultry have been perfected — hot smoking, cold smoking, and curing and smoking.

Hot Smoking

Hot smoking is a fairly rapid process that both cooks the meat and flavors it with smoke at the same time. The reason steaks and fish cooked over an open campfire taste so memorably good is because they are crudely "hot smoked." The slower the hot smoking process, the more intense the flavor. Hot smoking temperatures range from 85°F to 250°F. The delicious foods prepared this way should be eaten right away or kept under refrigeration less than a week.

Cold Smoking

Cold smoking is a long, slow process that can last weeks with temperatures never exceeding 85°F. Often just a trickle of smoke flows over the meat, very gradually permeating the tissue to give a mellow and delicate flavor. Cold smoked products keep for months.

Curing and Smoking

There are several ways to cure meat before smoking it, but the traditional methods are dry curing and brine curing.

Dry Curing. This is a salt dehydration process, now little used, that involves rubbing the meat with a mixture of salt, sugar, and often a small amount of sodium nitrate. Then the meat is stored at cool temperatures, allowing three days for each pound of meat. The salt gradually draws the moisture from the meat tissues. Large hams and bulky cuts often take longer than a month to cure. When the curing is finished, the meat is soaked a few days to draw off excess salt, air dried, then cold smoked. Food preserved this way is salty but almost indestructible.

Brine Curing. This involves soaking the meat in a pickling solution of salt, sugar, spices, and often a tiny amount of sodium nitrite at a rate of two to four days per pound. A six-pound pork shoulder takes about twenty-four days to brine cure; a big fifteen-pound ham must stay in the brine for two months. Often brine is injected along the bone of a big ham with a hypodermic needle. After the meat is cured, it may be soaked in fresh water a few days, dried, and then smoked.

Smoking cured meats improves their flavor immeasurably; the famous cured smoked hams of Virginia are testimony to this slow, careful process which makes hams, bacon, and sausages of premium quality.

Very often cured cold smoked meats, especially hams and bacon, are finished off at the end of the smoking period with a brief burst of hot smoking until the internal temperatures reach 140°F. Cured meats also can be hot smoked from the beginning at graduated temperatures for briefer periods than cold smoking demands, though gourmets and connoisseurs agree the results are not as fine.

An oven thermometer is a must for smokehouse equipment.

How Smokers and Smokehouses Work

The most efficient smoking is not done over a campfire, but in the confines of a closed shelter with a smoke source at one end and a vent at the other. Boxes, barrels, chimneys, old refrigerators, chicken houses, backyard barbecues, and tool sheds all have been converted into smokers or smokehouses successfully, though perhaps some of them shouldn't have been. A chicken house or a barrel that contained pungent substances, such as oil or detergent, imparts the flavor of the original use to the meat. It is vital to the final rich flavor to start out with a clean, neutral-scented smoker.

Old refrigerators, though often recommended as being easily converted into good smokers, have real drawbacks. The insulation often catches fire and ruins the meat being smoked; the plastic parts and chromed racks, when subjected to heat, give off toxic gases. The newer model refrigerators are almost completely plastic on the inside and dangerous to use as a smoker. Besides, a grimy, smoke-stained old refrigerator sitting in your backyard is something of an eyesore. It is better to build a permanent and attractive, sturdy smokehouse, or a box or barrel smoker that can be put away when the job is done.

The Parts of a Smokehouse

Vents. The smoker or smokehouse must have a top vent, or vents, not only to keep the smoke-laden air moving over the meat, thus drawing out moisture and evenly distributing the smoke, but also to prevent too dense an accumulation of smoke — and even soot and creosote — on the meat. A bottom vent near the smoke source helps control air, smoke, and heat flow over the meat.

Baffles. Baffles are useful in a smaller smoker; they force the smoke to take a slower, longer journey through the smoker, rather than a swift straight run from smoke inlet to vent. Baffles encourage an even dispersion of smoke through the enclosure, and wring the last drop of flavor from every wisp of smoke. Baffles also permit some measure of temperature control.

Racks and Hooks. Inside the smoker there should be adjustable pegs and hooks from which to hang the slabs of bacon, fish, sausages, hams, and the hens and turkeys in their net bags. Movable benches and racks are the place to lay the more tender fish fillets, or such fragile or small food as frogs' legs, woodcock, oysters, shrimp, and nuts.

Smoke. The smoke can come from a variety of green hardwoods, hardwood chips, or sawdust. Maple, hickory, apple, birch, ash, oak, and *dry* willow all give excellent flavor. The traditional smoke for hams is from green hickory wood and hickory sawdust. Corncobs can be used, but the smoke flavor is inferior to good hardwood.

Never, never use softwoods, such as spruce, pine, cedar or fir in a smokehouse — a black, sooty deposit, bits of flying ash, and a strong and unpleasant flavor of evergreen essence will ruin the meat. Experts advise not even using softwood kindling to get your smoke fire going, nor crumpled paper, nor any kind of starter or kerosene, for all of these impart their distinctive aromas to the meat and may contribute an unsightly residue of flying ash.

If you get hardwood sawdust from a furniture factory or woodworking mill, be very sure it is not from plywoods. In the smoke of such sawdust are evil-smelling, poisonous gases from the glue used to bind the plys together.

Rat-proofing. Covers and stoppers to fit the smoke and vent holes should be rodent-proof and left in place when the smoker is unused.

How to Make Smokers and Smokehouses

Here are four different smokers and smokehouses you can build — from a smoke pit to a permanent concrete smokehouse.

The box smoker and the barrel smoker are similar in function, but the box construction allows more control over smoke density and temperature simply by sliding the vent cover open or closed. A nongalvanized, nonchromed grill laid across the hanger racks allows you to smoke fish and other foods that must lie flat. These simple smokers should serve the needs of the family that raises only one pig or has an occasional lucky day fishing, or keeps a few chickens. Both have the advantage of being movable and can be stored when not in use, or left in place.

For the homestead or farm family with a good-sized poultry yard and livestock, or for the hunting-fishing family that regularly brings home venison, waterfowl, game birds, rabbit and hare, pike, salmon, and trout, a sturdy, permanent smokehouse that can hold up to twenty-four hams at a time is a good investment. In a rural community a neighborhood smoking project can preserve the meats of several families at once.

Making a permanent, well-constructed smokehouse is not a building project for someone who has never picked up a hammer before; some carpentry or masonry experience is very helpful. On the other hand, the project is both small enough and detailed enough to be an excellent learning experience preparatory to building your own house or barn. The key to success is to proceed slowly and carefully.

A slightly modified USDA plan for a concrete smokehouse is shown here. It is widely recommended because of its fire-resistant qualities, relatively low cost, and simple construction. However, if you find the concrete block smokehouse aesthetically unappealing, there are several alternatives. The concrete structure can be stuccoed or faced with brick or stone veneer. Another technique is slip-forming — pouring stone and concrete into forms for the walls — following the basic design given here. A Storey Publishing book by John Vivian, *Building Stone Walls*, will help you build it right. Not only is a stone smokehouse tight and durable, but it is handsome, a pleasure to look at and to use, and inexpensive if you have a good supply of stones.

Traditional smokehouses in the South were often log buildings. A small six-foot by eight-foot smokehouse goes up in a hurry, and can utilize leftover log ends from major log construction projects. Building a log smokehouse is an excellent training project before tackling a full-sized cabin or house. For a guide to working with logs, see Storey Publishing's book, *Build Your Own Low-Cost Log Home* by Roger Hard. Although softwood is the material of log builders, good-sized, seasoned, quaking aspen, or "popple," logs can be used for the smokehouse. This wood is now used by the building industry for studs, and if well-seasoned, gives good log-building results. Do not use hardwoods (with the exception of aspen). A log smokehouse should not be chinked with plastic material or fiberglass insulation. Use oakum, sphagnum moss, clay, or mortar.

Project 1: The Hot Smoke Pit

This extremely simple hole in the ground turns out delicious hot-smoked chickens, roasts, and fish. It is ideal for a Fourth of July picnic. (Be sure to surround the hole with a circle of temporary fencing to prevent anyone from accidentally stepping into it.)

The grill used in a hot smoke pit should not be galvanized or chromed. Half an old picnic grill or the grill from a hibachi is ideal.

Materials
flat rocks
vent rock
nongalvanized sheet metal for lid
nongalvanized grill
Tools
shovel

1. Dig a fire pit about 2' deep and wide enough to accommodate the grill.

2. Line the hole with flat rocks so that the grill is supported about 12" to 15" above the level of the coals.

Using the Hot Smoke Pit

Half an hour before starting the hot-smoke process, build a good hardwood fire in the fire pit, and let it form a bed of red hot coals. Then cover the coals with several handfuls of dampened hickory or other chips or small green hardwood twigs from apple, pear, maple, oak, or birch. Set the grill in place, and arrange the food to be smoked on the grill. Chickens will cook more rapidly if they are halved or quartered, but you lose much of the juices.

Put on the cover, adjust the vent rock under it to allow some smoke to escape. The narrower the vent opening, the more intense the smoke flavor, and the more slowly the meat will cook. The wider the opening, the more subtle the smoke flavor, the more rapid combustion (and heat) of the wood, and the higher the cooking temperatures. It will take the meat slightly longer to cook than in the kitchen oven — an additional 15–20 minutes for every hour.

You can put the food to be smoked on the grill with no preparation; sweet corn in the husk is very fine when hot smoked. Or you

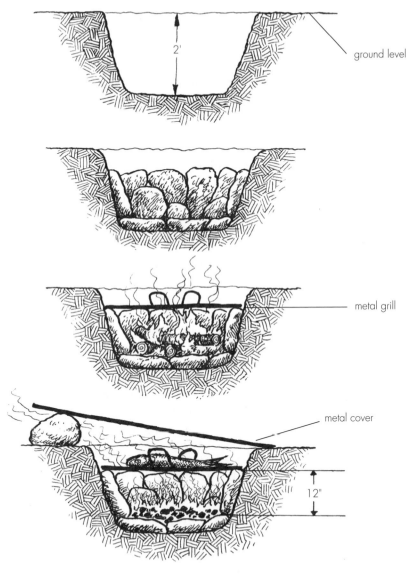

Figure 1. A hot smoke pit, dug 2' below ground level, lined with stone, and covered with a metal lid makes an ideal temporary smoker.

can marinate meat 4–6 hours in your favorite marinade. Here is a marinade recipe to try. It is especially good with chicken.

MARINADE

½	cup cider vinegar	1	clove garlic, crushed
½	cup hard cider *or* wine		ground pepper to taste
1	tablespoon salt		

Combine all the ingredients. Pour the marinade over the meat, fish, or poultry; cover and refrigerate. Turn the meat occasionally so that the marinade is distributed evenly. Marinate for 4–6 hours.

Project 2: The Barrel Smoker

This is a quickly and easily made cold smoker that can accommodate small amounts of food — two hams, four chickens, two turkeys, or whatever can be fitted in so that no piece of food touches another.

Materials

1 clean, 50 gallon barrel, wood or metal, with both heads removed
2 broom handles *or* 1" diameter poles
1 board: 1" x 10" x 10' *or* 11' of 6" stovepipe *or* drainage tile
1 piece of sheet metal: 3' x 3' *or* top of old metal drum
scrap lumber (approximately 1" x 4" x 14') for cleated barrel cover
   clean muslin *or* burlap to cover barrel top
1 large flat stone to cover the trench where it connects with fire pit
   (unnecessary if stovepipe or drain tile is used)
assorted flat stones
nails

Tools

hammer
shovel
tape measure
saw

1. Dig a fire pit about 2' deep and at least 18" across. Line it with rocks if necessary to prevent the earthen sides from collapsing. Dig a trench approximately 8" x 8" x 12' from the pit to the barrel location. The trench should rise about 1" per foot, sloping up from the fire pit.

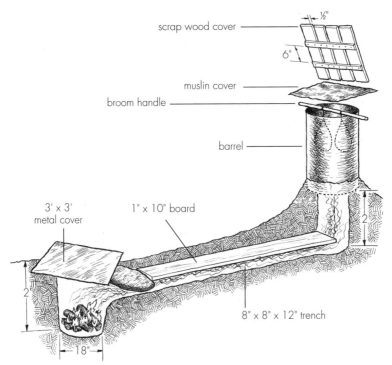

Figure 2. A barrel smoker can cold smoke small amounts of food.

Dig the smoke exit hole under the barrel-position-to-be. The hole should be about 2' deep and a little narrower than the diameter of the barrel. If you are working in loose, sandy soils, line the exit hole with flat stones.

2. Lay the large flat stone in place at the junction of the trench and fire pit if the board is used. The stone will protect the 1 x 10 from catching fire. Butt the board against the stone, and position it over the trench. (In sandy soils, you also may have to line the trench with flat stones.) Or lay smokepipe or drainage tile in the trench. If you use smokepipe, you can attach an elbow to the pipe to extend into the barrel.

3. Put the barrel in place over the smoke chamber.

4. Cover the board or trench liner with earth, and heap earth around the bottom of the barrel to prevent smoke from escaping.

5. Hang the meat to be smoked from the broom sticks and lay these across the barrel so the hams or turkeys hang down inside without touching each other.

6. Cover the top of the barrel with the muslin.

7. To build the barrel cover, measure the diameter of the barrel. Cut enough pieces from the 1 x 4 board or from scrap lumber to cover the barrel head, with a ½" space between pieces.

Cut 2 extra lengths. Lay these cleats on a flat surface, approximately 6" apart. Position the remaining lengths perpendicular to the cleats and nail together.

Lay the cover over the muslin. The 1" gap between the cover and the barrel edge caused by the broomsticks will allow excess smoke to escape.

Control the temperature and smoke volume by adjusting the barrel cover and the fire pit cover until the right level of heat and smoke is found.

Project 3: The Box Smoker

If you cannot find a clean, suitable barrel, or if you want a small smoker with a little more control, you can build a versatile smoke box in a few hours. Make it larger than a barrel for the increased capacity. A 4' x 3' box smoker is a convenient size that can take 6–8 hams at once, but you can vary the dimensions to suit your needs.

This box smoker is made from materials readily available from any lumberyard. To cut costs, you can use rough-cut boards or lumber from wooden shipping pallets.

Materials

Amount	Size
10 boards	1" x 6" x 8'
5 boards	1" x 6" x 12'
1 board	1" x 6" x 10'
4 boards	2" x 3" x 8'
1 board	2" x 3" x 10'
1 board	1" x 4" x 5'
1 board	1" x 3" x 10'
1 board	1" x 3" x 12'

¼ lb.	10d common nails
¾ lb.	6d common nails
⅛ lb.	8d common nails
40	1¼" wood screws
1	½" x 2' hardwood dowel
1	10–12' of 6" stovepipe
1 pair	2½" butt hinges and screws
1	hook and eye latch for the door
1	3' x 3' metal cover for the fire pit

Tools

shovel
saw
hammer
level
wood chisel
tape measure
T-square
screwdriver
brace and ½" bit
electric drill and bits

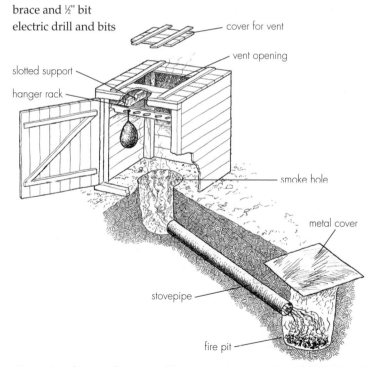

Figure 3. A box smoker can cold smoke twice as much as a barrel smoker.

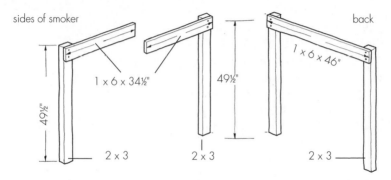

Figure 4. Assembly for back and sides of the box smoker (steps 1 and 2).

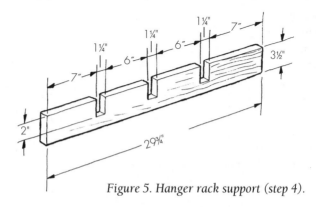

Figure 5. Hanger rack support (step 4).

1. To build the back of the smoke box, cut nine 1 x 6s to 46½". Cut two 2 x 3s to 49½". Lay the two 2 x 3s on a flat surface parallel to each other and 41½" apart. Between these, align the first 1 x 6 on top, flush with the sides and ends of the 2 x 3s.

Nail the 1 x 6 into place with two 6d nails. Position the second 1 x 6 edge to edge with the first 1 x 6. Align the ends with the outside edges of the 2 x 3s and nail into place. Continue until the nine boards have been nailed into the 2 x 3 corner supports. Set aside.

2. For each of the two sides, you will need nine 1 x 6 x 34½" pieces and one 2 x 3 x 49½" length. Lay the 2 x 3 on a flat surface. Perpendicular to it, align the first 1 x 6 with the end and outside edge of the 2 x 3. Nail together with two 6d nails.

Continue until the nine 1 x 6s have been nailed into place. (You may want to raise the other ends of the 1 x 6s with a scrap piece of 2 x 3 to make nailing easier.)

Complete the second side.

3. There will be runners along the top edge of each side to which the lid will later be nailed. Cut two 29¾" lengths from the 2 x 3 stock. Lay one of the sides flat on a work surface with the corner support facing down. Slip one length of 2 x 3 under the side so that it butts against and is perpendicular to the corner support. It also should be flush with the outside edge of the end board. Nail into place.

Follow the same procedure for the second side.

Cut one 2 x 3 to 41½". This runner will be nailed between the two back corner supports in the same manner.

4. Cut two hanger rack support boards to 29¾" from the 1 x 4 stock. Lay one of the pieces on a flat work surface. Measure in 7" from one edge and mark for a slot 1¼" wide and 2" deep. From the edge of the slot, measure in 6" and mark for a second slot. The third slot will also be separated by 6". This will leave 7" at the end of the board.

Saw along both sides of the slots to the 2" depth. With a chisel and hammer, chisel out the waste wood.

5. Screw the slotted supports on the inside of the side walls. The supports should sit on a line 12" from the top edge (the edge with the runner), and be screwed into place with 1¼" wood screws. Predrill the screw holes so that the wood doesn't split.

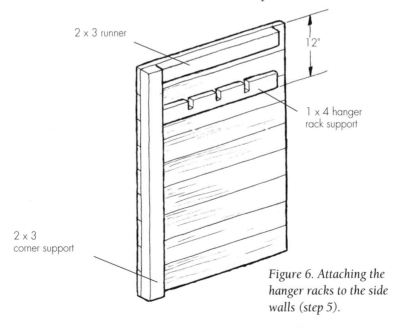

Figure 6. Attaching the hanger racks to the side walls (step 5).

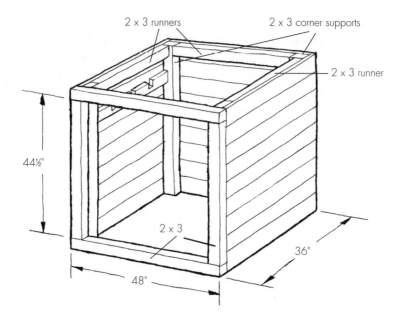

Figure 7. Box assembly (steps 7, 8, and 9).

6. Turn the back on edge so that it rests on one of the corner supports. Set one of the sides at right angles so that the sawn ends are flush with the outside of the back. Approximately 1⅛" in from the edge, nail each side board into the back corner support with two 6d nails per board.

7. Rotate the box so that the side rests on your work surface. Set the second side in place with its sawn ends flush with the outside of the back. Be sure the runners for the lid are opposite each other. Nail through the side boards into the back corner support.

You should now have a three-sided box with 2 x 3 supports in each corner. Set the box aside.

8. For the door frame, cut two 2 x 3s to 48" and two to 44½". Rest one of the 48" lengths on edge. Into it, toenail the shorter uprights, one at either end, using 8d nails.

Lay the second 48" length on edge. Tip up the U-shaped 2 x 3s so that the shorter uprights can be toenailed into the bottom cross rail.

9. Rest the three-sided box on its back. Set the door frame on top so that the top and bottom cross rails align with the outside edges of the sides. Measure in 1⅛" along the uprights and nail the frame to the corner supports with 10d nails.

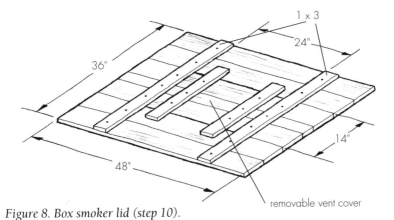

Figure 8. Box smoker lid (step 10).

10. The box smoker will have a cover and a movable vent cover. For the cover, cut four pieces of 1 x 6 to 48". Cut six pieces to 12", and rip two of these to 3" wide. Also cut two 1 x 3 x 36" lengths for the cleats.

On a flat surface, lay out the pieces so that the ends of three 12" lengths are 24" from the other three 12" lengths. (In each set of three there should be one of the 3" x 12" boards.) To the top and bottom of these, place two 48" lengths. There will be a 24" x 14" hole in the center for the vent.

To either side of the vent opening, place a 1 x 3 cleat. They should run perpendicular to the cover boards. Nail through the cleats into the lid boards with 4d nails. On the underside of the lid, bend over the nails with your hammer.

11. Place the lid on top of the box. Along the sides and back, measure in 1⅛" and nail the lid to the box corner supports and runners with 6d nails. Along the front, measure in ¾" and nail the lid down with 6d nails.

12. For the movable vent cover, cut three 1 x 6s to 24" lengths. Rip one to 3" wide. Also cut two 1 x 3s to 17" pieces. Lay the 1 x 6 boards edge to edge. Align the sawn edges. Perpendicular to the movable vent cover boards, equally space the two 1 x 3 pieces. Nail together with 6d nails. On the underside, bend the nails over with your hammer.

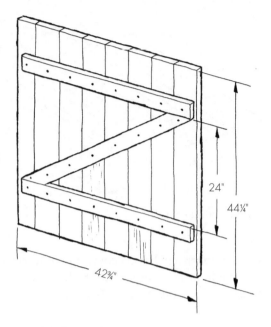

Figure 9. Door assembly (step 13).

13. Cut eight 1 x 6 boards to 44¼" lengths for the door. Rip one of the eight to 4¼" wide. Then cut two 1 x 3 boards to 42" long.

Lay the 1 x 6s edge to edge on a flat surface. Place the two 1 x 3 battens for the Z-brace perpendicular to the 1 x 6s, and 24" apart from inside edge to inside edge. Be sure they are centered on the door. Screw them into the 1 x 6s with 1¼" wood screws. Each board should be screwed top and bottom into the battens.

Measure for the 1 x 3 diagonal brace between the battens (approximately 48") and screw it into the vertical door boards.

14. Hang the door using the hinges, spaced about 5" from the top and bottom of the door. Screw into place and lift the door into the opening.

Put a piece of scrap lumber or a match book under the door to center it in the door frame. Mark the hinge placement on the smoker side edge. Remove the door and chisel out a slight depression to receive the hinge plate. Replace the door and fasten the hinges to the frame. Check that the door swings freely.

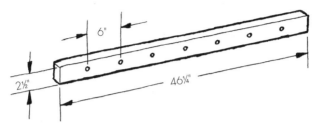

Figure 10. Hanger rack assembly (step 16).

15. Close the door. At a convenient height, screw an eye to the door frame and a hook to the door. This allows you to latch the door tightly.

16. Cut two hanger racks to 46¼" from 1 x 3 stock. They should fit between the slotted supports. Drill ½" holes 6" apart and at a slight upward angle for the dowels. Cut 3" dowel lengths and pound them gently but firmly into place.

Set the hanger racks into the slotted supports. Now the box smoker is ready to be positioned.

17. Locate the box smoker uphill from the fire pit. Dig a smoke hole, fire pit, and trench as for the barrel smoker. Place the smokepipe in the trench (or use drain tile or a board-covered trench) and cover with earth. Mound the earth around the base of the box smoker.

Project 4: Concrete Block Smokehouse with a Concrete Floor

Permanent smokehouses can be made of stone, logs, concrete, or wooden framing members, and should be large enough to meet the needs of an average family (usually a 6' x 8' x 8' structure). For these buildings, a concrete floor is necessary to protect the house from rodents, with concrete footings set below the frost line to insure a sturdy, durable structure. The fire pit, located outside the building, is vented through the floor into the smokehouse.

Experienced builders will have no trouble erecting a permanent smokehouse; less experienced builders may want to consult manuals on masonry and wood-framing techniques.

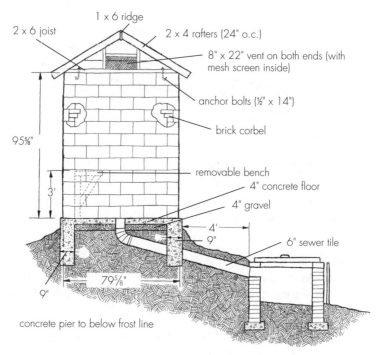

Figure 11. Concrete block smokehouse.

The Site

The site for a smokehouse should be at least 50' away from other buildings as a fire hazard precaution, especially if you will be building a frame structure. The firebox should be located at least 4' (preferably more) from the smokehouse. The drawings here are for only 4' of tile for the smoke channel; buy additional tile if your firebox is farther away. The firebox smoke hole should be lower than the smokehouse floor smoke hole to facilitate upward smoke movement; the optimum pitch is 30 degrees. Placing the smokehouse on a knoll is also helpful.

The foundation of both the smokehouse and the firebox should extend below the frost line for your area. (This may mean relocating your smokehouse if your soil is full of boulders.) In cold regions with a deep frost line, you will need more sand, gravel, and cement than specified in the list of building materials.

Only a concrete block smokehouse is described in detail; however, the design and foundation for any permanent smokehouse are quite similar (the exception: the foundation walls for the frame building are only 6" wide; for the concrete block building, they are 9" because of the additional weight of the walls). The rest of a log or frame building is erected according to standard building techniques.

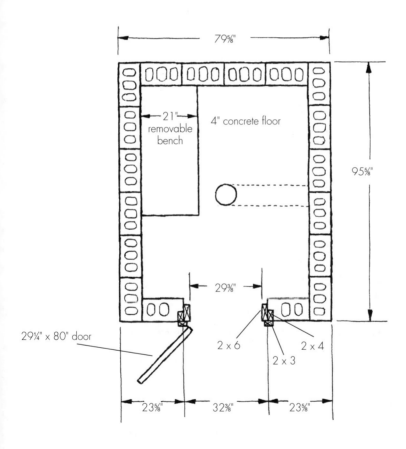

Figure 12. Concrete block smokehouse floor plan.

Materials

Masonry

Concrete: 1:3:5 mix of cement, sand, and gravel

Mortar: 1:3 plus 10% hydrated lime (in total: 14 bags of cement, 1½ cubic yards of sand, 2 cubic yards of gravel, and 65 pounds of hydrated lime)

Amount	Size
145	8" x 8" x 16" smooth face concrete blocks
12	8" x 4" x 16" smooth face concrete blocks for the corbel section
2	8" x 4" x 8" smooth face concrete blocks
14	8" x 8" x 8" smooth face half concrete blocks
52	8" x 8" x 16" corner concrete blocks
8	8" x 8" x 8" lintel blocks
10	8" x 8" x 16" jamb concrete blocks
10	8" x 8" x 8" half jamb concrete blocks
100	common bricks

Lumber

Amount	Size
12 boards	2" x 4" 8'
7 boards	2" x 4" x 10'
6 boards	2" x 4" x 6'
1 board	1" x 3" x 8'
4 boards	1" x 4" x 10'
1 board	1" x 6" x 6'
6 boards	1" x 6" x 7'
1 board	1" x 6" x 8'
1 board	1" x 6" x 10'
3 boards	2" x 3" x 8'
6 boards	2" x 6" x 7'
2 boards	2" x 6" x 8'
1 board	2" x 6" x 10'
3 pieces	1" x 3' hardwood dowels

120 square feet plywood or board sheathing for roof

1 roll roofing paper

shingles or roofing to cover 100 square feet

Miscellaneous

Amount	Size
8	4" lag bolts
10	½" x 14" anchor bolt with nuts and washers
1 pair	8" T-hinges
2 pairs	2" x 2" tension hinges

4 linear feet	#30 mesh screening 10" wide
⅓ lb.	6d common nails
¾ lb.	8d common nails
½ lb.	10d common nails
2 lbs.	16d common nails
¼ lb.	16d casing nails
20	2" wood screws

hanging hooks (optional)
stucco, stone, or brick facing (optional)
8' rebar
1 latch and strike plate
at least 4' of 6" sewer tile and elbow

Firebox
7 bags cement, ½ cubic yard sand, ⅓ cubic yard gravel
450 common bricks
90 firebricks
4 pieces ¼" steel rods 44" long
4 pieces ¼" steel rods 36" long
2 pieces 1¼" pipe 36" long
24" x 32" metal sliding door
24" x 48" light gauge metal strip
36" x 44" piece ¼" hardware cloth

Locating the Smokehouse

1. Decide on the exact location of the 79⅝" x 95⅝" smokehouse; then dig the foundation trenches to below the frost line. In firm soil, foundation forms aren't needed for the concrete walls.

2. Locate and mark off for the 44" x 52" firebox. Dig trenches for the fire pit to below the frost line.

Also dig a trench for the 6" tile, remembering to pitch it up towards the smokehouse. Join and place sections of tile in the trench. Attach the elbow so that the pipe will reach through the concrete floor and into the smokehouse.

Cover the floor surface of smokehouse with 4" of ½" gravel or broken stone.

3. Pour concrete footings for smokehouse and firebox; let harden. Then level the gravel layer on the smokehouse floor, plug the tile opening with a metal or wooden ring stopper, and pour a 4" concrete slab.

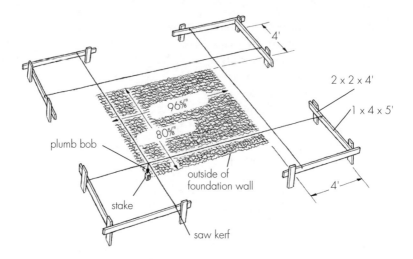

Figure 13. Mark off the four outside coroners of the foundation wall. Then erect batter boards. Run masons cord between the batter boards and adjust until the line accurately outlines the foundation. Check that the lines are level and the corners are square. Building lines are removed during excavation but can be replaced whenever necessary (step 1).

Firebox Cover

4. The firebox cover is made of concrete. Build a 36" x 44" form from 1 x 6s. Nail the form together and lace on level ground. Along the inside, draw a line 1" down from the top edge. Add a ½" sand bed in the bottom of the form to make it easier to remove the slab after the concrete has hardened.

5. From the 24" x 48" metal sheet, cut a semicircle 48" in outside diameter and 36" in inside diameter. You can improvise a compass with a nail, a 30" piece of string, and a magic marker. Rivet the ends of the strip together so that it forms a circle with a 24" diameter and tapered sides. Stake this in the center of the form.

6. On the top of the sand, lay the hardware cloth (you will have to cut an opening for the tapered metal circle). Twist short sections of wire at the joints to lock the reinforcing rods in place, and fit the grid around the metal circle. Let grid rest on top of the hardware cloth.

Dampen the sand and pour in concrete until it reaches the line along the inside of the form; do not pour any concrete into the center circle. Allow to harden; then remove the form and metal circle.

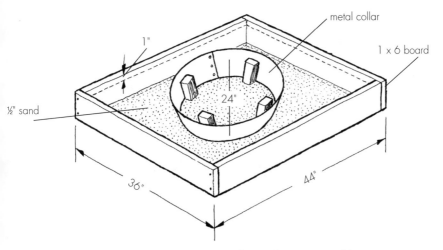

Figure 14. The firebox cover is made of poured concrete and leaves an opening for a lid to control combustion rates (step 4).

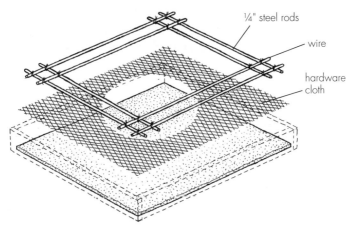

Figure 15. The firebox cover is reinforced with ¼″ steel rods (step 6).

7. Use the metal circle to separately cast a 4" concrete lid. Place a sturdy metal handle in the center before the concrete hardens. Once cured, the tapered concrete plug should fit neatly into the center of the concrete lid.

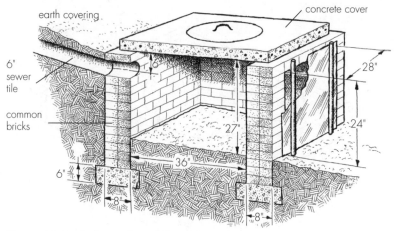

Figure 16. Smokehouse fire pit (step 8).

The Fire Pit

8. Lay up the walls from the footings to the fire pit with common bricks. Thereafter use firebricks for the inner row. A 24" x 28" door opening must be left for access to the fire pit. On top of the firebox, center the 36" x 44" concrete cover and cement into place.

Smokehouse Walls

9. Lay up eight courses of concrete blocks on top of the smokehouse foundation walls. Remember to alternate between jamb and half jamb blocks around the doorway; the 2" x 4" indentation on these blocks is for the door framing which will be added later.

10. Being the ninth row from the doorway and work to either corner. Down the sides set 8" x 4" x 16" blocks on edge and flush with the outside edge of the wall. Mortar the brick corbelling into place on the remaining interior lip. The corbelling makes a strong continuous ledge for the removable 2 x 4 hangers to rest on.

11. Frame the doorway. Some jamb blocks come with predrilled holes to accept lag bolts. If so, use lag bolts to fasten the 2 x 4s to the block walls on either side of the doorway. If you have blocks without predrilled holes, drill them yourself using a mortar bit. Then attach with lag bolts.

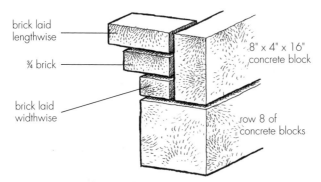

brick laid lengthwise

¾ brick

brick laid widthwise

8" x 4" x 16" concrete block

row 8 of concrete blocks

Figure 17. Corbel detail (step 10).

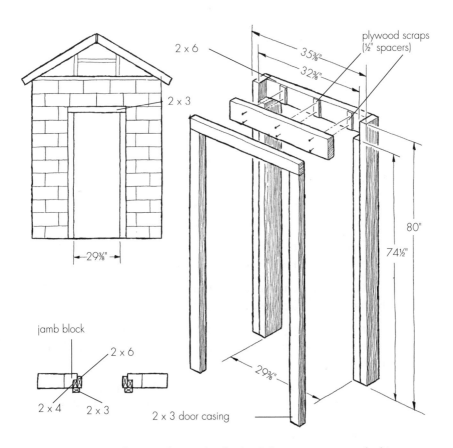

2 x 6

2 x 3

plywood scraps (½" spacers)

35⅞"

32⅞"

29⅞"

80"

74½"

jamb block

2 x 6

2 x 4   2 x 3

2 x 3 door casing

29⅞"

Figure 18. Door framing (step 11). The 2 x 3 door casing is attached in step 18.

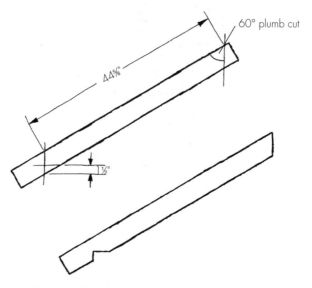

Figure 19. Rafters cuts (step 13).

Continue laying up the eleventh and twelfth tiers of concrete blocks, setting a lintel of eight lintel blocks and two sections of rebar, each 48" long, over the doorway.

12. After the top tier of blocks has been laid, set the anchor bolts in place. Bolt the 2 x 6 top plate to the concrete walls.

13. To frame the roof, use 2 x 4 x 5' rafters with a 60° plumb cut and spaced on 24" centers. Nail these into the 1 x 6 x 10' ridge.

14. On both gable ends of the smokehouse, there will be a 8" x 22" vent. Frame these using scrap 2 x 4 stock.

15. Cut three 2 x 6 joists to span the distance between the two side walls; they will sit on the top plate. Nail joists into second, third, and fourth sets of rafters.

16. Blocking is necessary before the fly rafters for the overhang can be nailed into place. Cut twelve 2 x 4s to 10½". Nail these to the existing end rafters at 1' intervals from the ridge. Then nail fly rafters into ridge and into blocking.

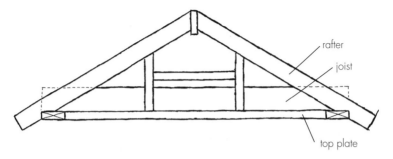

Figure 20. The joists are nailed to the rafters. Joist tops will have to be trimmed to match the angle of the roof pitch.

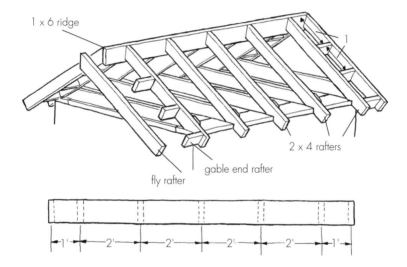

Figure 21. Nail the fly rafters into the ridge and into the blocking attached to the end rafters (step 16).

The Roof

17. There are different roofing materials available, such as asphalt shingles, hand-split cedar shakes, and metal roofing. You may want the smokehouse roof to match that of your house, or you may have access to leftover roofing materials. The most common method is to sheath the roof with plywood, and cover with felt paper and asphalt shingles.

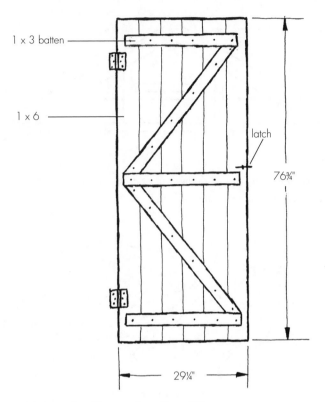

Figure 22. Board and batten door (step 19).

The Door

18. Align the 2 x 3 casing pieces flush with the outside edge of the door framing and nail into place.

19. Build a 29¼" x 76¾" board and batten door out of 1 x 6 and 1 x 3 stock. Mount the hinges 8" from the top and bottom of the door, and lift door into place. Predrill and screw hinges to frame. Then mount the latch and strike plate.

Vent Doors

20. Trim the vent door opening with 2 x 3s. Cut two pieces of plywood to 8" x 22" and hinge to top trim piece using the tension hinges.

Around the inside of the vent opening, staple the wire screening to keep out insects. Close in gable ends with plywood.

Hanger Racks

21. To span the distance between the brick corbelling on the interior side walls, cut six or as many 2 x 4 x 71" hanger racks as you will need. The hangers can be pegged with 1" doweling as in the Box Smoker rack hangers.

For greater capacity in your smokehouse, suspend a tier of lower level hangers on an additional support instead of building the removable bench.

Bench

22. If desired, construct a bench along one wall. Most useful may be a slotted bench of hardwood strips to hold small or delicate foods that cannot hang.

Finishing Touches

23. Heap earth over the tile. Drive two sections of 1¼" pipe into the ground in front of the firebox opening. Slide the metal door into place, and the smokehouse is ready for use.

24. When using the smokehouse, always open the firebox door with a long-handled poker.

The gable vents are opened from the inside with a long pole; the tension hinges will hold them open at the desired angle.

Sources

Directions for butchering, dressing out livestock and game, curing, and smoking everything from chicken livers to kippered herring can be found in a number of books. Some of the best are listed here. Also check Extension Service Web sites for food preparation information.

Ashbrook, Frank G. *Butchering, Processing and Preservation of Meat.* New York: Van Nostrand Reinhold, 1974.

Eastman, Wilbur F. *A Guide to Canning, Freezing, Curing, and Smoking Meat, Fish and Game.* North Adams, MA.: Storey Publishing, 2002.

Mettler, John J. *Basic Butchering of Livestock and Game.* North Adams, MA.: Storey Publishing, 2003.

Sleight, Jack and Raymond Hull. *Home Book of Smoke Cooking Meat, Fish & Game.* Harrisburg, Penn.: Stackpole Books, 1988.